60th Birthday Edition

Dr. Seuss's
THE
CAT
IN THE
HAT
Sticker Activity Book

Hi! I'm the Cat in the Hat. It's my birthday – and it's time to play! With stickers to stick and things to colour, this book has fun like no other... So what are you waiting for? Let's get started!

TM & © Dr. Seuss Enterprises, L.P.
All rights reserved

3 5 7 9 10 8 6 4 2

ISBN: 978-0-00-821962-8

Copyright © 2007, 2017 Dr. Seuss Enterprises, L.P.

Published by arrangement with Random House Inc., New York, USA
First published in the UK in 2017 by HarperCollins Children's Books.

Some of the materials in this book originally appeared in slightly different form in
The Cat in the Hat 50th Birthday Sticker Activity Book and The Cat in the Hat 50th Birthday
Colouring and Activity Book: TM & © 2007 Dr. Seuss Enterprises, L.P. 1957

HarperCollins *Children's Books*

It's a cold, wet day and the children are stuck in the house.

Who is looking out of the window? Can you find them in your stickers?

Sally and her brother can't play with their toys indoors.

Can you find three outdoor toys in your stickers? Use the clues to help you.

Something you throw – what is it?

You can sail this on a lake.

This is fun to ride around on.

Then... something
went BUMP!

Fill in the blanks to find out who is
stepping in on the mat. Then find the
right-shaped sticker to see if you are right!

The/cat in/The/hat

HERE COMES THE

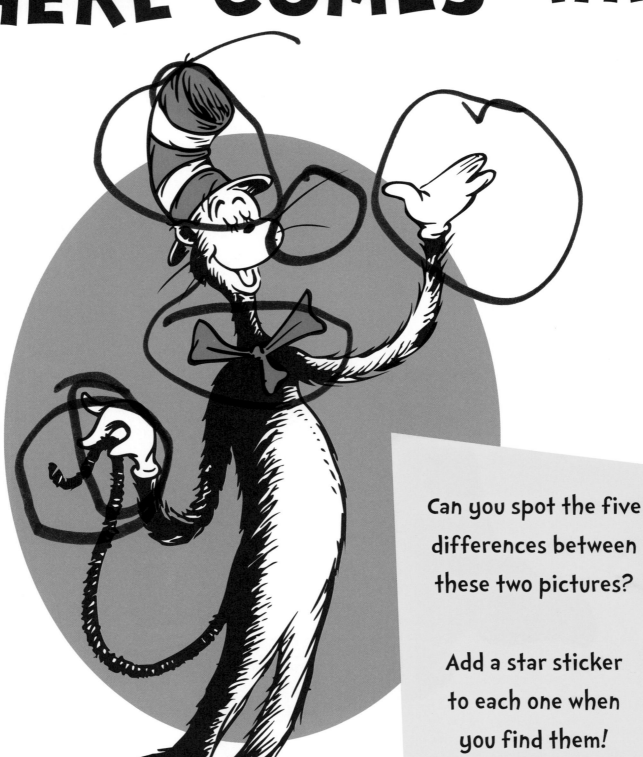

Can you spot the five differences between these two pictures?

Add a star sticker to each one when you find them!

CAT IN THE HAT!

The Cat in the Hat is showing how many things
he can balance while standing on a ball.

Use your stickers to complete the balancing act!

Now can you copy this picture into the space using the grid to help you?

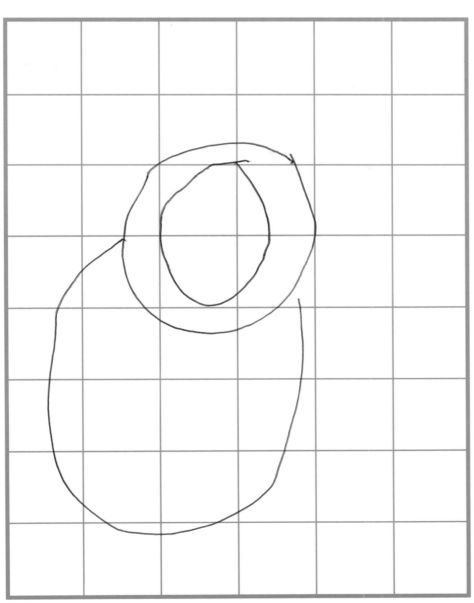

The fish is worried that the Cat in the Hat will fall and make a mess. Help the children through the maze so they can rescue the fish before the Cat in the Hat falls!

What else is the
Cat in the Hat balancing?
Use your stickers
to find out!

Oh no, the Cat's taken a tumble.
Don't forget to add in the fallen
down rake and umbrella stickers!

Join the dots to see
what else he's dropped
and then colour in
your drawing!

What a mess! Can you find the right pieces
to complete the puzzle with your stickers?

The Cat in the Hat has brought something new to play with! Follow the wiggly lines from each object to find out which ones are inside the box.

Things One and Two have come to play but they do make a mess. They have hidden these words every which way in this box. Can you find all the words in the wordsearch? Look up, down, side to side, diagonally and back to front! Mark each one off the list with a sticker when you find it.

THINGS
ONE
TWO
FISH
TEAPOT
KITE
TOY
GOWN

PLAY
MESS
UMBRELLA
PICTURE
LAMP
DRAWERS

Page 2

Page 3

Page 11

Page 5

Pages 6-7

Page 8

Page 12

Page 14

Page 16

Pages 24-25

Pages 18-19

Pages 28-29

Page 31

B	R	R	B	H	S	I	F	C	P
U	Z	U	O	N	E	J	B	P	I
M	U	M	T	P	E	Z	B	M	C
E	M	E	H	L	T	O	Y	A	T
T	B	M	I	T	O	G	F	L	U
I	R	R	N	A	W	L	O	D	R
K	E	O	G	N	J	O	A	W	E
F	L	B	S	Y	A	L	P	E	N
M	L	T	E	A	P	O	T	F	G
P	A	P	D	R	A	W	E	R	S
M	J	M	E	S	S	N	S	P	E

18

The Things are flying kites in the hall and are getting up to all kinds of bad tricks.

Use your stickers to find out what has got caught up on the kite strings.

Thing One and Thing Two are making such a mess that they must be caught and put away. Play this game with a friend and see how many Things you can catch!

HOW TO PLAY

* Take turns to join a pair of dots horizontally or vertically, somewhere in this grid. When you complete a square shape, put your initials inside. Each complete square is worth 1 point.

* If you complete a square with one of the Things inside, you get double points!

* When all the squares are drawn, the winner is the player with the most points.

* When you have finished, you can play again on the opposite page!

Thing One and Thing Two are still on the loose.
Help the children catch them by drawing a big net!

The Cat in the Hat has gone but he has left a big mess. Help Sally and her brother to find each of these items in the pile so they can tidy up. Add a star sticker to each item when you find it!

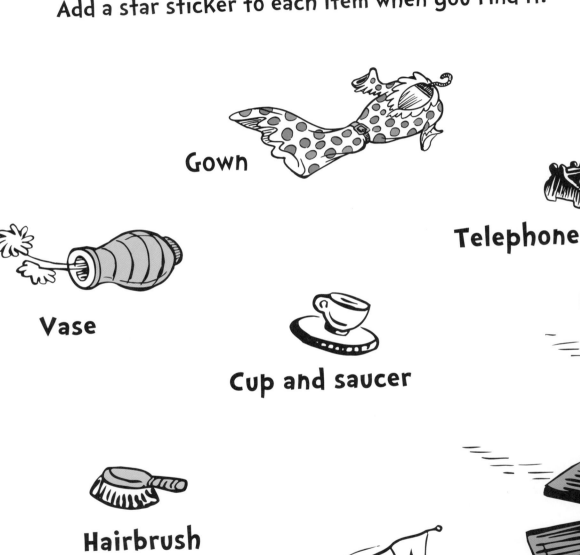

Gown

Vase

Cup and saucer

Telephone

Hairbrush

Fan

Rake

The fish has no need to worry –
the Cat always picks up his playthings.
Colour in the Cat in the Hat and his
cleaning-up contraption.

The Cat in the Hat has cleaned almost
everything up, but there are a few
more things to be put back in place.
Use your stickers to help complete the picture.

The Cat in the Hat has left one last puzzle to solve.

Use the wiggly lines and your stickers to pair up
each character with their partner or belonging.

Answers

Pages 6-7

Page 14

Page 15

Page 16-17

B	R	R	B	H	S	I	F	C	P
U	Z	U	O	N	E	J	B	M	I
M	U	M	T	P	E	Z	B	A	C
E	M	E	H	L	T	O	Y	L	T
I	B	M	I	T	O	G	F	L	U
K	R	R	N	A	W	L	O	D	R
E	O	G	N	J	O	A	W	E	N
F	L	B	S	Y	A	L	P	E	N
M	L	T	E	A	P	O	T	F	G
A	P	D	R	A	W	E	R	S	S
M	J	M	E	S	S	N	S	P	E

Pages 10-11

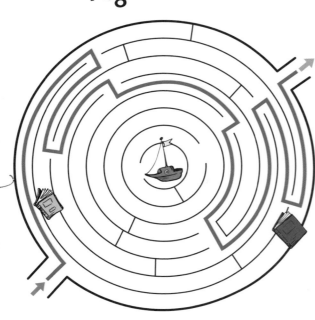

Page 24-25